Welcome to the

Ready to see our real farm in action?

We prepared videos for you to
immerse yourself in our dairy farm.
Open your camera and hoover over the QR code below,
click the link that appears and be prepared to
watch, listen, and learn.

I hope you are inspired to learn more about
farm life and to go after one of your dreams.
To learn more about farm life, check out
Malecha Enterprises YouTube channel.

Louise Malecha

Praise for *Going to Papa and Nana's Farm*

"*Going to Papa and Nana's Farm* by Louise Malecha allows readers to enjoy a realistic and engaging view of the workings of a dairy farm. This book is beautifully illustrated by the author's daughter, Katelynn. Young readers will have lots of fun as they ride along with Papa on his giant farm tractor! Nana will take them with her on a visit to see a newborn calf, and to watch the cows being milked. This book is a treasure for children of all ages."

~ Joanette Weisse
International bestselling author of the *Giggles in my Heart* series

"This engaging and fact-filled book by Louise Malecha is both affectionate and informative, and the irresistible illustrations created by Louise's daughter, Katelynn, are bursting with color and personality. *Going to Papa and Nana's Farm* is certain to catch and keep the attention of children for many generations to come!"

~ Judy O'Beirn
Founder & President, Hasmark Publishing International

"*Going to Papa and Nana's Farm* by Louise Malecha is a story of the workings of a modern-day dairy farm and how the animals are protected, cared for, and fed. This book will surely broaden the perspective of any young city child who may have only seen farm animals or machinery from the car window. I must admit, I was also enlightened—I did not know that cows were milked three times a day in the parlor!"

~ Shaaron Fedora
International bestselling Author of *Twigs in My Ears* and *The Loneliest Teddy Bear*

"Simply put, this is a delightful book with a sweet storyline and beautiful illustrations. The brightly coloured pictures seem to jump off the pages and tell the story all by themselves. I really love how the book incorporates so many themes, from family and spending time outdoors, to learning about a working farm and the love of animals. It is a wonderful book for children to look at by themselves, as well as for adults who wish to share the experience of reading with their children and grandchildren."

~ Sarita Howart
International bestselling author of *Dash the Cheeky Dachshund Visits the Farm*

"There is nothing better than seeing a working farm come to life through the eyes of a child. Louise Malecha and her daughter Katelynn have done a masterful job of capturing the fun, excitement, and diversity of living and working on a dairy farm. I've actually had the privilege of visiting Papa and Nana's farm in real life, and it is as delightful as the book portrays it to be. *Going to Papa and Nana's Farm* is a must have!"

~ Rena Striegel
President, Transition Point Business Advisors

To our seven children who have grown up around the farm and still, to this day, love the family life. To our grandchildren who are always curious when it comes to what happens on the farm.

Today is a very special day for Sadie and Jack.

"Wake Up! Wake Up! It's time to go!" says Sadie. She bursts into Jack's room.

Acknowledgements

Emily Malecha for her help and input on the book.
Katelynn Malecha for her creativity in her beautiful pictures.
Rena Striegel for her encouragement to write the book.
Thank you.

Jack sits up in bed and rubs his eyes.

"Where are we going?" asks Jack.
"We are going to Papa and Nana's farm!" says Sadie.
"We will have so much fun!"

"In the car we go," says Sadie and Jack's mom.

"We don't want to be late. Are you sure you packed your boots, Jack?" asks Mom.
"I sure did. I even brought Timmy, my turtle!" says Jack.

Mom drives them to Papa and Nana's farm.

"I see lots of pretty trees and plants!" says Sadie. "The air smells so fresh, like daisies."

This is Papa and Nana's Farm.

**This is one of Sadie and Jack's favorite places to go.
It has big barns for the cows and little houses for the calves.**

A lot of things happen on the farm.
Cows are milked and fed. Lots of care is given to the calves.

Tractors, loaders and other farm machines are fixed, cleaned and used to make food for the animals.

"What do you want to see today?" asks Papa.

"I want to see the calves!" says Sadie as she hugs Nana.
"I want to see the tractors!" says Jack as he runs to Papa.

"Jump on!" says Nana. "I will take you to see the cows and the calves."

Sadie and Jack hop on the cart. They enjoy rides.
Spud, Papa and Nana's dog, jumps on the cart with them.
He likes rides, too.

Nana takes care of the cattle. She has workers to help her.

They help her take special care of the animals. The animals are fed good food every day.

Cal, one of Nana's helpers, drives the tractor.

Cal pulls a mixer behind the tractor to spread hay, corn and lots of good stuff for cows. Sadie and Jack run their hands through the feed. "Mmm. It smells so good," says Jack.

Sadie and Jack watch the cows being milked.

"This cow is brown. Does it give chocolate milk?" asks Sadie.
"No, all cows give white milk," laughs Nana.

"Nana, how many times a day are the cows milked?" asks Jack.

"The cows are milked three times a day," says Nana. "They are happy to come to this big room. It is called a parlor."

"Where are the calves?" asks Sadie.

Nana takes them to see a newborn calf.

"This calf was just born minutes ago," says Nana.

Sadie and Jack pet the calf.
"It's a girl!" says Sadie. "She has a soft, warm coat."
"We will feed her milk and give her a cozy bed," says Nana.

"Let's go see Papa!" says Nana.

"Where is Papa?" asks Jack.
"I have a good idea," says Nana. They all climb onto the cart to find what Papa is up to.

Papa is working in the shop.

"What are you doing, Papa?" asks Sadie.
"I am cleaning and shining this tractor.
Do you want to help?" asks Papa.

Sadie and Jack pick up brushes to scrub the tractor.
They both get a little dirty, but they have fun.

"Who wants a ride in the tractor?" asks Papa.

"We do!" shout Sadie and Jack. Sadie goes first. She has a smooth ride with Papa.

Jack has a bumpy ride. Bump! Bump!

Papa and Jack ride across the field to check the irrigator. It's like a giant sprinkler that waters the corn and hay in the field.

Papa pulls something out of his pocket.

"What is it, Papa?" ask Sadie and Jack.
"Oh! It's a bag of jelly beans!" laugh the children.

Sadie and Jack say good-bye to Nana and Papa.

It has been a very fun time for them on the farm.
They can't wait to come back for their next adventure.

For more information, please visit:
www.louisemalecha.com
www.malechainc.com
Instagram: Louise Malecha
Facebook: Louise Malecha
louise@malechainc.com

About the Author and Illustrator

Louise Malecha is "Nana" to her grandchildren. She grew up on a dairy farm with her thirteen siblings. With her husband, Todd, they raised their seven children in the agricultural lifestyle teaching them strong work ethic and leadership. She now enjoys when she can bring her grandchildren's imagination to life by showing and teaching them activities on their farming operation as she did her own children. Teaching, mentoring, and health and fitness are strong passions of hers.

Katelynn Malecha is the daughter of Louise Malecha. She grew up working, playing, and occasionally getting into mischief with her six siblings on the farm. Growing up, one of her responsibilities was to tend to and take care of the calves, which has taught her responsibility and hard work. She continues to be a part of the family operation doing anything from driving equipment to illustrating her mother's book. Photography, graphic design and agriculture are some of her strong passions.

With every donation, a voice will be given to the creativity that lies within the hearts of our children living with diverse challenges.

By making this difference, children that may not have been given the opportunity to have their Heart Heard will have the freedom to create beautiful works of art and musical creations.

Donate by visiting

HeartstobeHeard.com

We thank you.

Made in the USA
Columbia, SC
02 April 2025